BRITISH COLUMBIA
ALPHABET BOOK

NICKY BIRD

iThink Books

Arbutus trees have reddish brown bark that looks like it is peeling off.

Aa

A is for arbutus

A B C D E F G H I J K L M N O P Q R S T U V W X Y Z

The **bald eagle** eats mostly fish. These birds are often found near water.

B b

B is for bald eagle

A pair of bald eagles uses the same nest for many years. They add new sticks to it every year.

Young eagles are dark brown. They get a white head and tail when they are about four years old.

The largest gathering of bald eagles in the world happens every winter near Brackendale.

C c

C is for caribou

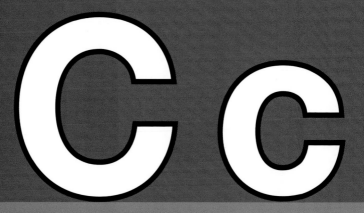

Caribou are a kind of deer.

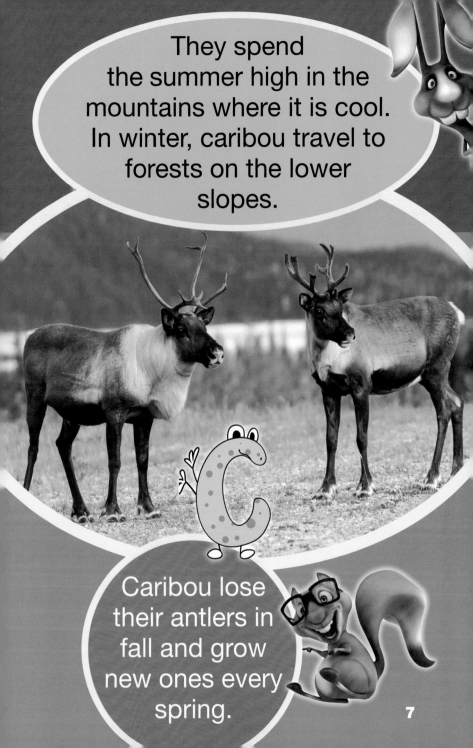

They spend the summer high in the mountains where it is cool. In winter, caribou travel to forests on the lower slopes.

Caribou lose their antlers in fall and grow new ones every spring.

7

A
B
C
D
E
F
G
H
I
J
K
L
M
N
O
P
Q
R
S
T
U
V
W
X
Y
Z

Dd

D is for dogwood

Pacific **dogwood** is the official flower of British Columbia.

8

The white flowers bloom in spring. This shrub has bunches of red berries in fall. You can eat the berries, but they are bitter.

Indigenous peoples used branches from the dogwood to make bows and arrows.

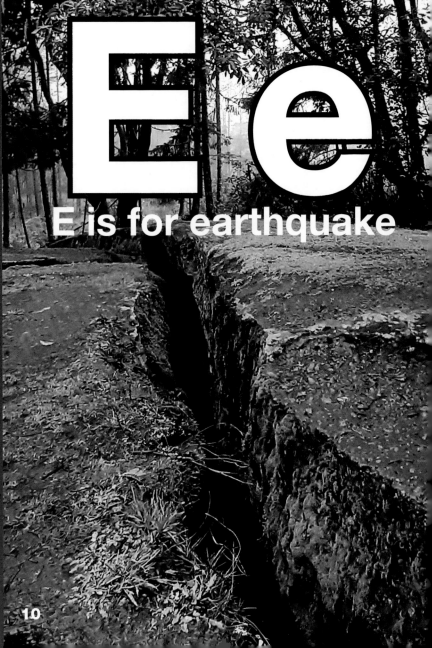

Earthquakes often shake the coast of British Columbia.

Ee

E is for earthquake

A B C D **E** F G H I J K L M N O P Q R S T U V W X Y Z

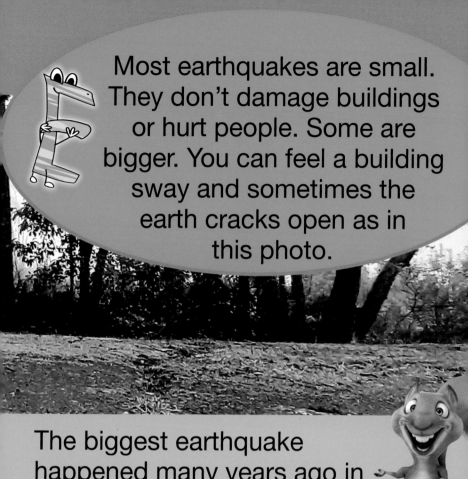

Most earthquakes are small. They don't damage buildings or hurt people. Some are bigger. You can feel a building sway and sometimes the earth cracks open as in this photo.

The biggest earthquake happened many years ago in Haida Gwaii. Buildings were damaged, but no one died.

A
B
C
D
E
F
G
H
I
J
K
L
M
N
O
P
Q
R
S
T
U
V
W
X
Y
Z

The **Fraser River** is the longest river in British Columbia. It starts near Mount Robson and flows across the province to Vancouver and the Pacific Ocean.

Ff

F is for Fraser River

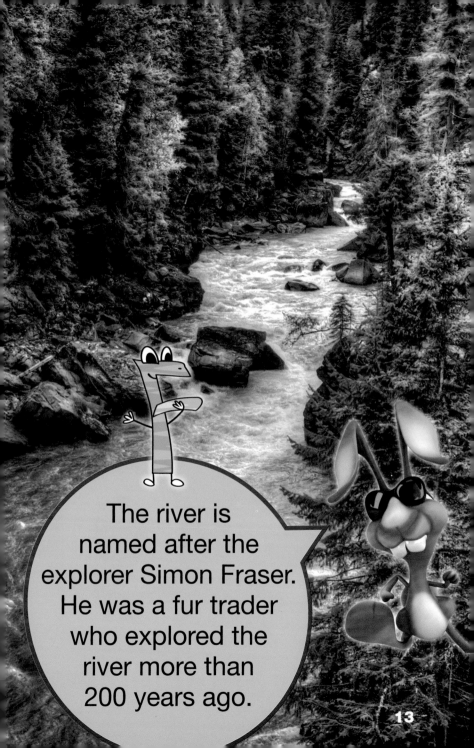

The river is named after the explorer Simon Fraser. He was a fur trader who explored the river more than 200 years ago.

Gg

G is for glacier

Glaciers are large, thick sheets of ice. From far away they look like snow.

They flow like very slow-moving rivers. Most glaciers move only a few centimetres per day.

British Columbia has thousands of glaciers high in the mountains.

Hh

H is for Haida Gwaii

Haida Gwaii is a group of islands on the northern coast. The name means "islands of the Haida People."

Many of the plants and animals on the island cannot be found anywhere else.

The Haida people made these beautiful totem poles. Some of them were made to guard a village.

17

I i

I is for Ice Man

Not long ago hikers found the mummified body of a young Indigenous man.

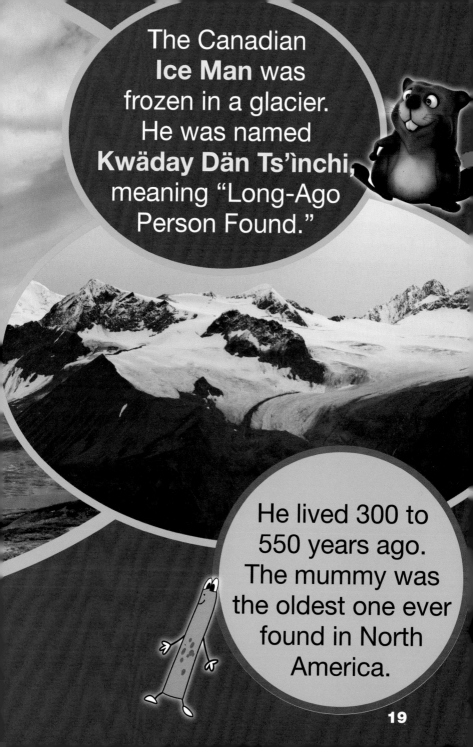

The Canadian **Ice Man** was frozen in a glacier. He was named **Kwäday Dän Ts'ìnchi**, meaning "Long-Ago Person Found."

He lived 300 to 550 years ago. The mummy was the oldest one ever found in North America.

A B C D E F G H I J K L M N O P Q R S T U V W X Y Z

Jade is the official gemstone of British Columbia.

J j

J is for jade

Jade is a hard green stone.

The gemstone is found mostly in the northern part of the province.

21

A B C D E F G H I J **K** L M N O P Q R S T U V W X Y Z

K k

K is for Kermode bear

The **Kermode bear** is a rare kind of black bear that is white.

It is sometimes called **spirit bear** or **ghost bear.**

Kermode bears live in rainforests along the coast.

23

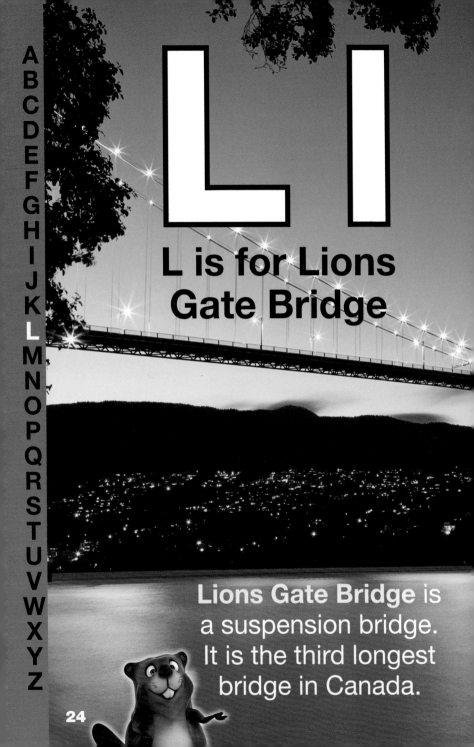

L l

L is for Lions Gate Bridge

Lions Gate Bridge is a suspension bridge. It is the third longest bridge in Canada.

A B C D E F G H I J K L M N O P Q R S T U V W X Y Z

It connects Vancouver with the north shore of the Burrard Inlet.

The bridge is named for a pair of nearby mountain peaks.

Mm

M is for
Mount Robson

Mount Robson is the highest mountain in the Canadian Rockies. It is 3954 metres high.

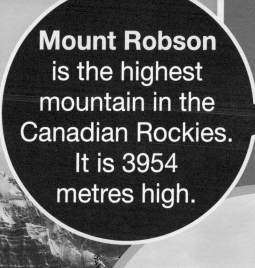

It is so high that the top is often hidden by clouds.

Visitors like to hike up or around the mountain.

ABCDEF GHIJKLM NOPQRSTUVWXYZ

British Columbia has seven **national parks**. That's more than any other province.

Nn

N is for national parks

The parks are Glacier, Gulf Islands, Gwaii Haanas, Kootenay, Mt. Revelstoke, Pacific Rim and Yoho.

x

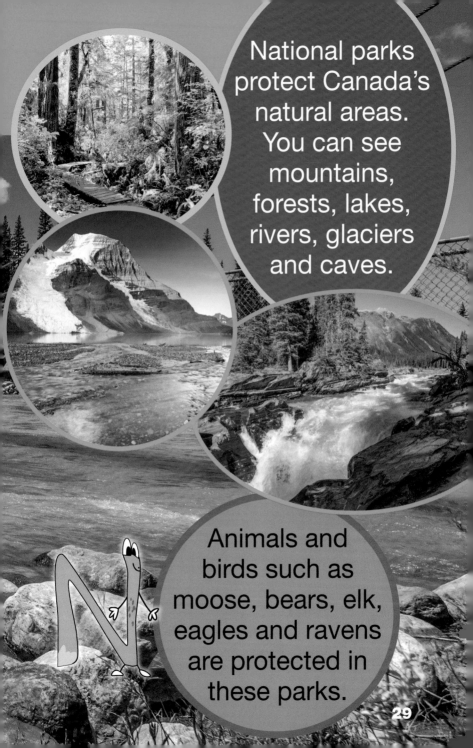

National parks protect Canada's natural areas. You can see mountains, forests, lakes, rivers, glaciers and caves.

Animals and birds such as moose, bears, elk, eagles and ravens are protected in these parks.

29

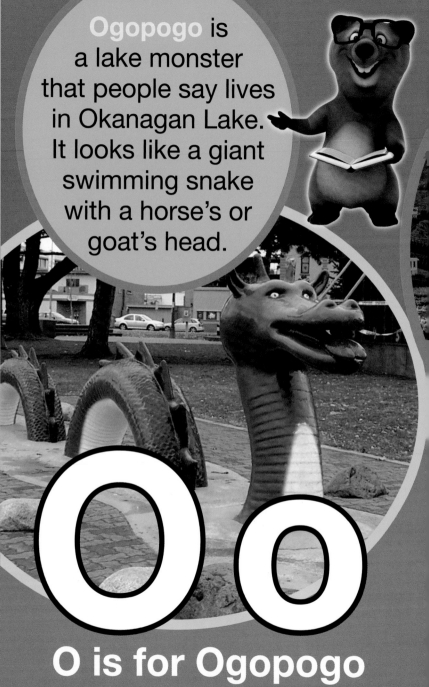

Ogopogo is a lake monster that people say lives in Okanagan Lake. It looks like a giant swimming snake with a horse's or goat's head.

A B C D E F G H I J K L M N O P Q R S T U V W X Y Z

O is for Ogopogo

Many people say they have seen Ogopogo. No one is sure if it is real.

The **Peace Arch** is a monument. It is on the Canada–United States border near Surrey.

PEACE ARCH PARK

BRITISH

COLUMBIA

B.C. PARKS

Pp

P is for Peace Arch

33

Quesnel is a small city in central BC.

Qq

Q is for Quesnel

It was named after fur trader Jules-Maurice Quesnel.

The town was the centre of the Cariboo Gold Rush from 1862 to 1865.

When you say **Quesnel**, the letter **s** is silent.

ABCDEFGHIJKLMNOPQRSTUVWXYZ

Rr

R is for raven

The **raven** is an important bird to Indigenous culture.

It is one of the smartest animals. Some ravens can even learn to talk.

Ravens sometimes work together to hunt larger animals.

S s

S is for salmon

Seven kinds of **salmon** live on the west coast: Chinook, coho, pink, sockeye, steelhead, cutthroat and chum salmon.

Salmon hatch from eggs laid in a river. The young salmon swim to the ocean.

When it is time for the female salmon to lay her eggs, she returns to the river where she hatched. This is called a **salmon run**. Millions of salmon swim up BC rivers each spring.

Tt

T is for Takakkaw Falls

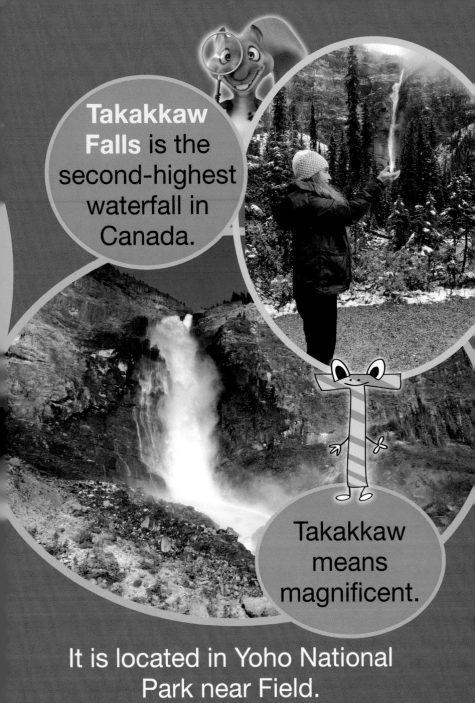

Takakkaw Falls is the second-highest waterfall in Canada.

Takakkaw means magnificent.

It is located in Yoho National Park near Field.

Uu

U is for urchin

Sea **urchins** are small, spiny creatures that live on the bottom of the ocean.

You can see them in tidal pools along the coast. The purple sea urchin is the most common.

Urchins eat kelp, a kind of seaweed.

A B C D E F G H I J K L M N O P Q R S T U V W X Y Z

Victoria is the capital of British Columbia. Victoria is on Vancouver Island.

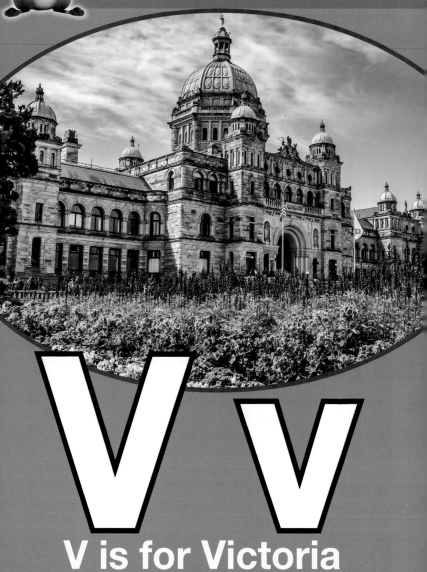

Vv
V is for Victoria

To get there, people often travel by ferry. A ferry is a big boat that carries cars and people.

Victoria is one of the oldest cities in western Canada. The city was named after Queen Victoria.

Whistler is a town in the mountains north of Vancouver.

Ww

W is for Whistler

In winter, people go there to ski and snowboard. In summer, you can go mountain biking.

Whistler hosted many events in the 2010 Winter Olympics.

ABCDEFGHIJKLMNOPQRSTUVWXYZ

YA TI SLQILH ST'ILAA XAYCAP ULH NUXALK

Xeni Gwet'in is a First Nation.

Xx
X is for Xeni Gwet'i

Yy

Y is for Yoho National Park

Yoho is a small national park near the BC–Alberta border.

It has many beautiful mountains, lakes, such as Lake O'Hara, and waterfalls, such as Takakkaw Falls.

The Burgess Shale is in the park. It holds many interesting fossils.

The Burgess Shale

51

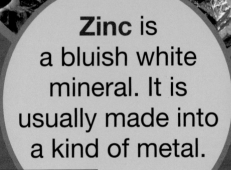

A B C D E F G H I J K L M N O P Q R S T U V W X Y Z

Zinc is a bluish white mineral. It is usually made into a kind of metal.

Z z

Z is for zinc

There are many zinc mines in BC. A long time ago, there was even a town called Zincton.

Zinc is used to cover steel and iron objects so they don't rust.

Canada has more zinc deposits than anywhere else in the world.

Games and Puzzles

Can you **find 7 differences** between these two pictures?

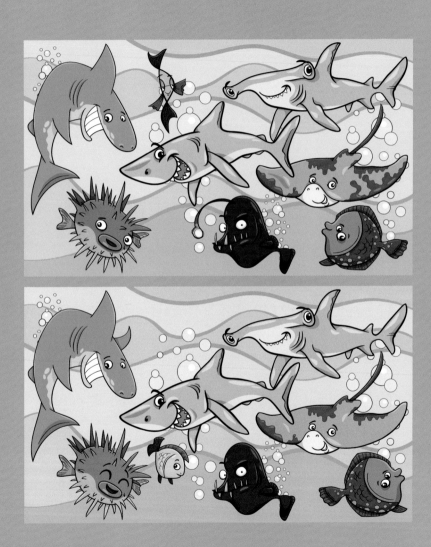

Sea creature crossword.

Games and Puzzles

Follow the path to help the fish find his friend.

How many? Count the similar sea creatures and write the number in the box below.

Games and Puzzles

Forest animals word search

E	B	E	A	R	K	F	N	E	S	J
T	E	P	G	S	B	L	E	T	N	R
N	A	M	T	R	X	H	R	S	A	E
O	U	W	O	L	F	C	A	N	S	E
O	T	A	R	S	B	N	H	A	P	D
C	N	Y	D	B	M	V	S	K	N	E
C	R	S	Q	U	I	R	R	E	L	A
A	G	F	E	R	T	J	B	H	C	X
R	F	C	B	E	A	V	E	R	A	O
A	S	D	U	O	L	F	C	B	X	F
F	H	E	D	G	E	H	O	G	S	E

Game and puzzle answers.

Find the Differences, p. 54

1. dolphin   2. octopus   3. turtle
4. anglerfish   5. narwhal
6. shark   7. whale   8. seahorse
9. crab

Crossword, p. 55

Count the similar sea creatures, p. 57

Follow the Path, p. 56

F	H	E	D	G	E	H	O	G	S	E
A	S	D	U	O	L	F	C	B	X	F
R	F	C	B	E	A	V	E	R	A	O
A	G	F	E	R	T	J	B	H	C	X
C	R	S	Q	U	I	R	R	E	L	A
C	N	Y	D	B	M	V	S	K	N	E
O	T	A	R	S	B	N	H	A	P	D
O	U	W	O	L	F	C	A	N	S	E
N	A	M	T	R	X	H	R	S	A	E
T	E	P	G	S	B	L	E	T	N	R
E	B	E	A	R	K	F	N	E	S	J

Word search, p. 58

59

Do you remember what British Columbia word goes with the letter and the picture?

A a

B b

C c

D d

E e

F f

G g

Hh
Ii
Jj
Kk
Ll
Mm
Nn

Oo

Pp

Qq

Rr

Ss

Tt

Uu
Vv
Ww
Xx
Yy
Zz

The Publisher: iThink Books
iThink Books is an imprint of Folklore Publishing Ltd.

Library and Archives Canada Cataloguing in Publication

Title: British Columbia alphabet book / Nicky Bird.
Names: Bird, Nicky, 1961– author.
Description: First edition.
Identifiers: Canadiana (print) 2020025829X | Canadiana (ebook) 20200258303 | ISBN 9781897206256 (softcover) | ISBN 9781897206263 (EPUB)
Subjects: LCSH: Alphabet books. | LCSH: English language—Alphabet—Juvenile literature. | LCSH: British Columbia—Miscellanea—Juvenile literature.
Classification: LCC PE1155 .B56 2020 | DDC j421/.1—dc23

Photo credits: Every effort has been made to accurately credit the sources of photographs and illustrations. Any errors or omissions should be reported directly to the publisher for correction in future editions.

Front cover credits: GettyImages: Scott Canning
Back cover credits: GettyImages: AndreaKuipers, Kimberly Nesbitt. Wikipedia: Hamedog

Photo Credits: GettyImages: 6381380, 5; A_Melnyk, 46; AlvaroRT, 52, 63; AndreaKuipers, 8, 60; Anne08, 18, 61; avagyanlevon, 21, 61; Eduardo Baena, 39, 42; berkay, 21; bgsmith, 13, 60; blizzard87, 15; blublaf, 47; bluejayphoto, 44, 45, 63; bmswanson, 27; bobloblaw, 6, 60; canbalci, 45; Scott Canning, 22, 61; CreativeNature_nl, 36; davemantel, 3; dutourdumonde, 10; Ryan Djakovic, 10, 60; William Dummitt, 29; EHStock, 45; emer1940, 9; enifoto, 29; Eric_Z, 24; FloWBo, 56, 59; Derek Galon, 39; gbh007, 47; GlowingEarth, 29; moose henderson, 4, 60; Alena Igdeeva, 58, 59; jamesvancouver, 33, 62; Valdas Jarutis, 43, 63; JeannaThacker, 29, 61; JessieEldora, 49; jonmccormackphoto, 23; kavram, 51; lucky-photographer, 51; Markpittimages, 40, 62; Marina_Poushkina, 50, 63; miroslav_1, 26, 61; MriyaWildlife, 37; Nachosan, 51; natchapohn, 57, 59; naturediver, 2, 60; Kimberly Nesbitt, 17, 61; Tomas Nevesely, 14, 60; Thomas Northcut, 25, 61; PaulReevesPhotography, 5; photoworks1, 32; ppa5, 46, 63; pschoenfelder, 37, 62; redfishweb, 19, 48, 63; reisegraf, 15; rightholder, 43; Mark Robertson, 41; ronniechua, 23; S-S-S, 55; Murphy_Shewchuk, 17; SciPhiTV, 9; slovegrove, 53; SMJoness, 31; Volkantg, 3; Luen Wantisud, 20, Wirepec, 41; witoldkr1, 38, 62; Igor Zakowski, 54, 59. *Wikipedia:* Benoit Brummer, 34, 62; Daily Mail, 31; Frad Dally, 35; Hamedog, 30, 62.

Animal Illustrations: julos/Thinkstock.

Letter Illustrations: mariaflaya/Thinkstock.

Produced with the assistance of the Government of Alberta. Alberta Government

Funded by the Government of Canada
Financé par le gouvernement du Canada | Canadä

We acknowledge the financial support of the Government of Canada.
Nous reconnaissons l'appui financier du gouvernement du Canada.

PC: 38-1